MW00718551

LIFE
IS GIFT

LIFE
IS GIFT

HENRY E. ROBERTS

ARDARA HOUSE, PUBLISHERS

PENSACOLA, FLORIDA

LIFE IS GIFT

Library of Congress Catalog Card Number: 94-78068

ISBN: 0-9637647-7-2

To the congregation of The First United Methodist Church of Pensacola, Florida, my family of faith for the past decade; to those living; to those who have gone before us into the life beyond; and to those who will come after us to serve the cause of Christ in this place.

TABLE OF CONTENTS

PROLOGUE

✤

Running easily over the grass at the side of the blacktop road, I could see far out over the waters of Escambia Bay. The water was a little choppy and gray, reflecting the early morning rain clouds. It was the Saturday before Labor Day, 1993. I was preparing my body and mind for the grueling task of running in the New York City Marathon in October. Headed north on Scenic Highway, I ran as always well to the shoulder and facing on-coming traffic.

I love the water and the views of Escambia Bay. My mind soared with the gulls as I was carried on the wind. I breathed deeply of the humid September air and let the rhythm of my serene thoughts match the deep rhythmic breaths: "Life . . . is . . . really . . . good . . . ."

* * * * * * * *

I became aware of relentless pain before I could open my eyes to see where I was — pain in my head, pain in my legs, pain in my arms, pain in my back. I became conscious of blinding light and various noisy medical machines, of hovering faces and careful hands.

"What happened . . . ? Where . . . ?"

I learned that I was in the Intensive Care Unit at Sacred Heart Hospital. It was late Saturday afternoon. They told me briefly that a sleepy early-morning driver had allowed her car to drift from the northbound lane all the way across the southbound lane to the roadside where I was running. The car slammed into me from behind, with no warning. The projecting bumper shattered my lower legs first, then catapulted me backwards, up and over the hood, so that the back of my head struck the glass of the windshield, and I flipped over the top of the car. From there, nobody knows.

Life . . . is . . . really . . . good.
Life . . . is . . . .

Chapter I

❖

Life is GIFT

"At fourteen, Andrea Jaeger won her first professional tennis tournament. At eighteen, she reached the finals of Wimbledon. At nineteen, an injury to her right shoulder all but ended her career. Now, at twenty-eight, no longer able to compete on the professional tennis circuit, she serves little kids instead of aces."

This is *Sports Illustrated*'s report (May 16, 1994) of the former tennis champion who founded and maintains a nonprofit organization that attempts to bring some joy to children who are suffering from cancer or other life-threatening illnesses. Andrea Jaeger runs it full-time, year-round, unpaid.

"I'm inspired by these brave kids, and humbled," says Andrea. "They lose their health, their friends and sometimes their lives. And yet their spirit never wavers. *They look at life as a gift.* The rest of us sometimes look at ourselves as a gift to life."

They look at life as gift. That is a vital insight, one that we understand as children but often lose as we grow to maturity. I have come again to realize that all of life comes to us as gift. Before we are even a gleam in our parents' eyes, we are a thought in the mind of God.

> *It was you who created my inmost self, and put me together in my mother's womb; You know me through and through, from having watched my bones take shape when I was being formed in secret, knitted together in the limbo of the womb.* (Psalms 139:13-15)

Frederick Buechner, in *Listening to Your Life,* says that a great theologian, after lecturing learnedly on miracles, was asked to give a specific example of one. "There is only one miracle," he answered. "It is life."

Then Buechner asks:

Have you wept at anything during the past year? Has your heart beat faster at the sight of young beauty? Have you thought seriously about the fact that someday you are going to die? More often than not do you really listen when people are speaking to you instead of just waiting for your turn to speak? Is there anybody you know in whose place, if one of you had to suffer great pain, you would volunteer yourself?

If your answer is "no" to all or most of these questions, says Buechner, the chances are that you're dead.

As a person who has recently had a narrow escape from death, I will tell you something. My answer to most of these questions is "Yes! Yes! Yes!" The reason is that I am so aware now — on a daily, sometimes on a moment-by-moment basis — that life is gift, a very precious gift.

That gift has several dimensions that we are likely to take for granted.

For one thing, we have been given the privilege

of being citizens of the United States of America. I didn't, because of great wisdom, pick the United States out of a lineup of family-of-nation possibilities. My U.S. passport came as a birthright. Just as easily I could have been born a citizen of Rwanda or Somalia or any of a dozen other third world countries.

Instead, I am a part of the American family. Life's urging for itself created me and placed me in my mother's womb and birthed me in this place. My life in this nation is a gift. And here I am provided with opportunity to learn and work hard, limited only by my vision, shaped by my dreams. Place of birth is a dimension of life that for me has provided multiple blessings.

Another gift aspect of life for me is that ever since I can remember, there have been persons around me who have been strong and wise, loving and supportive — during my formative years my mother, my father, my brother. My wife Jane, also, has taught me the sustaining truth that Life is Gift. Jane's spiritual depth, self-giving life style, her beauty and health and soundness of mind have guided and strengthened my life for over thirty years. Sometimes, knowing what I now know about life, I feel as if I have won the lottery with my choice of a marriage partner.

Mary McMillan is another who understood the gift of life. Mary became a gift to the people of Japan, serving as a missionary there for thirty-four years. Only six months before Mary died, a young Japanese girl came with a tiny baby to a Sunday morning worship service in Mary's home church, where I am pastor. I never know who may show up as God's gift of the week! That day this very well-mannered Japanese woman just appeared. No one in the congregation had seen her before. After the service she introduced herself to me as Mitsuko Igushi, bowed politely, and left. That was that, I thought, but the next Sunday she was back with her beautiful baby. I spoke to her after the service. "Thank you very much," she said as she smiled. To my questions she responded in broken English, but for the most part all she said was, "Thank you very much." Finally I asked her if she understood what I was saying as I preached. Her reply was, "Thank you very much!"

That Sunday afternoon I telephoned Mary at her childhood home near Pensacola, where she was living in retirement, to tell her about the Japanese girl, and thus was initiated a relationship that would last until Mary's death.

Mitsu spoke at Mary's memorial service. She told how "Teacher Mary" had given her so much "comfort and encouragement." Mitsu spoke of her respect for all Mary did for the people of Hiroshima. Also, she was grateful for the time Mary had spent teaching her English. She shared with us a couplet Mary had used with her as she had with her pupils in Japan: "Though Love is weak and Hate is strong, yet Hate is short and Love is long."

Soon after Mary's death, Mitsu came to see me to say, "I must go back to Japan." I have missed her and often I have thought of her. I never really understood why she was in Pensacola and why she went back to Japan. Sometimes I have wondered if perhaps she was an angel that God sent to be here when Mary died, to help us all realize that Teacher Mary belonged both to us and to the Japanese people. Mary was a gift, with us but for a little while. And Mitsu was a gift, as well.

The gift of relationships can be felt in the entire network of persons who help bear us along in life. Awareness of the "presence" of all these persons came to me after emergency surgery which held the possibility of saving my right leg after the accident. With modern drugs most of the pain can be handled, but for my body, a mixture of morphine and a drug for nausea called *phenergan* became a deadly combination, slowing my body's ability to pump blood and exchange air, a pair of pretty necessary activities. When severe respiratory problems resulted, the doctors switched to a codeine drug.

In the fog of all of this medication, I began to see some interesting phenomena on the walls of the hospital room — drawings, script, and faces. Nothing scary, like a Spielberg movie, but very confusing. I would tell the doctors about it when they checked on me, and each time they ordered a battery of tests: an MRI, nerve conduction tests, and nuclear x-rays — and always they would draw blood! After a time, I began to wonder if I might not die of all the tests!

I finally realized that every time I mentioned something that I was seeing, I was sent for another test, so I just stopped talking about it. I mean, I am slow, but eventually I catch on!

Soon the script and drawings all disappeared, but the faces remained. Some of the faces I recognized, but most I did not. They were not scary faces and neither were they happy faces. Concerned and very attentive, they watched me with an intensity I had seldom experienced. Although the faces went away eventually, there still remains to this day the awareness that I was being watched over, cared for, prayed for, and loved. What a wonderful and unexpected gift!

While I wonder at my being the object of attention from these hovering hosts, I marvel at the feeling that God is a presence, as well. The Psalmist expresses such wonderment:

> *When I look at your heavens, the work of your fingers, the moon and the stars, which you have established; What are human*

beings, that you are mindful of them?
Mortals, that you care for them? Yet you
have made them a little lower than God,
And crowned them with glory and honour.
You have given them dominion over the
works of your hands . . . . (Psalms 8:3-6)

Since last September's Labor Day weekend, I continue to affirm that God is mindful of me as he is for every person and facet of his creation. If, indeed, I have some degree of "dominion over the works of [God's] hands," then how grateful I am for the gift of the Holy Spirit as I set about doing what needs to be done, about living life!

Harry Haines, former head of United Methodist Committee on Relief, wrote to me: "Isn't it wonderful to discover that God isn't through with you yet?"

Joshua Loth Liebman said that "We live today with the everlasting arms beneath us. We breathe, we eat, we walk, we think and dream, all because we are sustained by a universe greater than ourselves and preserved by a love beyond our fathoming."

Andrew Young writes in his recently published

spiritual memoir, *A Way Out of No Way*:

> *I have begun continually to look for the hand of God in my daily life. I have come to believe that God truly is with us. God is with our children and with our parents. God is with our friends and our enemies. God is with our business partners and with our competitors. In retrospect, events that seem accidental or even tragic at the time of occurrence turn out to be more developments in God's continuously unfolding and marvelously meaningful plan.*

There is a sense in life of being mysteriously protected, of being watched over and cared for. It is a sense that is shared by M. Scott Peck and expressed in his book, *Further Along the Road Less Traveled:*

> *How in God's name that protection works, I have no idea except that it somehow is in God's name. In my office I have the figures of seven different angels hanging around in various states of disrobement. The reason they are there is not because I have ever seen*

a humanoid creature with wings, but when I come to contemplate the mechanics of this protection, the mechanics of grace, how God can seemingly literally count the number of hairs on our heads (which in my case is becoming less of a responsibility for Him these days) I can only imagine Him having armies and legions of angels at His command.

Some might ask the imponderable: if God sends his ministering angels to keep us safe, why didn't God on that September day protect me a little more? The truth is, I believe he did. One of the many wonderful cards which I received was one addressed in an adult hand to "Preacher Henry," the name I am called by the children of the congregation. The childish scrawl inside read: "Dear Creature Henry, aren't we glad you were not hurt in the head."

Given the severity of the blow, my life could have easily been more drastically altered. I thank God that I was not "hurt in the head." Through experience I have come to believe that we have minimum protection but maximum security. And today, although I am not yet able to walk, I am dancing inside, for I know that God is with us.

I have always been aware that God was with me in the successes, the experiences of victory, when health was in abundance and I was singing, *O what a beautiful morning! O what a beautiful day! I've got a beautiful feeling! Everything's going my way!*

The mistake we make is to assume that we have earned or deserve or possess forever the good gifts which come our way. They can go away as swiftly as they have come, and they will! They can be lost as quickly as an unguided car can cross a road. Life is never to be owned or possessed or completely controlled.

I now know that when the nights get dark, when my days are filled with uncertainty and the future is a question mark, when I move through the valley of the shadows, God comes to me when I need him most.

The presence of many individuals during this year have given evidence of God's loving and supportive presence. Herb Sadler, a minister friend of many years, would inevitably appear to pray with me when I was ready for surgery, whether I was in my hospital room or the corridor. Once he showed up to pray at the entrance to the operating room!

But one day I received a telephone call from Herb saying that he would be out of town when surgery was scheduled and could not be with me. A fleeting thought came: Who would pray with me?

Early on the day of operation, just as the sun was coming up and the nurses were finishing their preparatory work, the door to my room opened, and Dr. Kirby Turnage, my orthopedic surgeon, quietly came in. After the usual greeting, I mentioned that he had come quite early for this surgery. He said, "I have come to have prayer with you."

He offered a most beautiful prayer for guidance and healing, and I learned once again the lesson that we are never alone in this world and that God always comes to us in our time of need.

For years I had mumbled through the words of the Twenty-third Psalm, but I now read it with tears of joy in my heart: *Yea, though I walk through the valley of the shadow of death, I will fear no evil, for thou art with me.* Even in death God will be with me.

I was recently privileged to hear Dr. Elizabeth Kubler-Ross, the renowned and respected scientist who has studied more than almost anyone else the subjects of death and dying. She has tested and analyzed hundreds of patients who have had near-death experiences, and her conclusion is that we never die alone. Your loved one may not be beside you when you die, but you are not alone. Someone is there.

John Wesley said on his death bed in his eighties: "The best of all is God is with us." I have found his witness to be true.

Terry Waite, a prisoner of Arab terrorists in Lebanon, was kept in solitary confinement for four years. He writes of his lonely experience in the autobiographical work entitled *Taken on Trust*. His only communication from the outside world was a postcard from someone he did not know. At one of the places he was imprisoned there was a peephole through the metal door. There was not much to see, but each day he could look through the tiny opening and see an elderly woman, who came out on a balcony to hang out her laundry. He could not speak to her, but he watched this evidence of ongoing life and began to feel, in the midst of his total isolation and loneliness, less alone. Lonely, yes, but never alone. He began to understand life differently. The gift of Life is the gift of the Presence of God.

As a friend and I discussed this concept of Life as Gift, we read together what the influential but pessimistic philosopher Arthur Schopenhauer wrote. The world, he said, is something which ought not to exist; the truth is that we have not to rejoice but rather to mourn at the existence of the world. It is absurd, he continues, to speak of life as a gift, as so many philosophers and thoughtless people have done. It is evident that everyone would have declined such a gift, Schopenhauer concludes, if he could have seen it and tested it beforehand.

All that is in me challenges that conclusion of Schopenhauer's. Even in the midst of my pain and suffering I became aware of life — of love and community, of people, and of God as Holy Spirit. During the time of struggle I have never been ready to decline the gift of life nor to mourn the existence of the world I know.

I wish Schopenhauer could have experienced his life joyfully, could have felt the power of revitalizing relationships, could have witnessed the lives of some of the people I have known, and could have felt the presence of the living Christ in his life.

Whatever life is, however bad it gets, there is a great anthem which sings in my soul. I heard it in the silent void of shock when I learned that an entire section of the tibia in my leg was missing. It soared in a song of gratitude when those who loved me came to express their caring. It sounded sweetly when those trained in the mysteries of orthopedics ministered to me. It brushed my hands when caring nurses and technicians touched me to register their assurance. It lingered as my daughters read to me the letters which came from hundreds of friends. It touched me when pain awakened me in the middle of the dark and lonely night, and Jane and I would laugh and cry together. I wouldn't decline that song, that gift of life, for all the learned discourses of all the pessimistic philosophers in the world.

Sometimes the gift comes in surprising sizes and shapes. When I was about eight years old, a very small child came to live in our home. His parents, members of our church, went to stay with his older brother who was dying of leukemia in a hospital in Birmingham. So Dusty came to live with my family. At first the arrival of the baby was an invasion of my territory, but it wasn't long before Dusty became *our* baby, like *our* car or *our* dog. When we went to sleep, *our* car was in the carport, *our* dog was by the front porch, and *our* baby was in his special room.

One day, after about a year, I came home from school and Dusty wasn't there. The Pritchetts, his parents, had come to get *our* baby. Their other child had died and they returned home to pick up the pieces of their lives and raise Dusty. I was mad, hurt, confused, lonely, depressed. They had come and taken *our* baby. But my mother, a very sensitive person who was dealing with those same feelings in a more acute manner than the rest of us, sat me down and put things in perspective. She said, "Look, you must remember, Dusty was never our baby in the first place. The fact that we ever got to enjoy him and take care of him at all was a gift. So, instead of being mad at his being taken away, let's be grateful that we had him at all."

Years later I would read in Khalil Gibran's book, *The Prophet,* that "Your children are not your children. They are the sons and daughters of Life's longing for itself. They come through you but not from you, and though they are with you yet they belong not to you." As I watched the years claim our daughters, I have remembered Dusty.

Years ago when our children were small, as we ended a very full day of celebration for our daughter's birthday, she said: "Daddy, we have had quite a day today, haven't we?"

I thought, you are right, we really have.

And that is true for me today. If it all ends today we have had quite a life. And the important thing is, every day of every year has come to us as gift.

Chapter II

Life is CHOICE

To my office recently came a woman in mid-life. As we talked, she revealed that she was feeling unloved, unlovable, unemployable, inadequate. I hurt for her and sought to counsel her as best I could. It seemed to me that somehow she had chosen Schopenhauer's negative outlook — that life is the kind of gift that would have been declined if it could have been seen and tested beforehand. What a difference a sense of Life as Gift would have made in that woman's life!

The Gospel of John tells the story of another person who would have been helped by a change in perspective, by a different understanding of life. Near the Sheep Gate in Jerusalem there was a pool (in Hebrew called *Bethesda*) with five porticoes. Sick people — blind, crippled, paralyzed — were on these porches, for legend held that from time to time an angel stirred the waters and that whoever stepped into the water first would be healed. Of course, we may properly regard that as mere superstition, but the people of the time believed it, and so the sick, the lame, and the blind gathered there. The Gospel of John tells us that Jesus spent a part of a day in the midst of this pathetic scene.

> *One man had been an invalid there for thirty-eight years. When Jesus saw him stretched out by the pool and learned how long he had been there, he said, "Do you want to be made well?"*
>
> *The sick man answered him, "Sir, I have no one to put me into the pool when the water is stirred up; and while I am making my way, someone else steps down ahead of me."*
>
> *Jesus said to him, "Stand up, take your mat and walk." At once the man was made well, and he took up his mat and began to walk.* (John 5:1-9)

Joe Elmore's paraphrase of this scripture, in his

book *This Fleeting Instant,* offers rare insight into Jesus' understanding of the invalid and his view of life:

> *Jesus called to a sick man, "Hey, sick man by the pool, do you want to get well?"*
>
> *"Get well? I can't get well. When the magic water stirs, somebody gets in before me — if only they wouldn't do that . . . if only I could move faster . . . if only the water stirred more often . . . if only . . . . Get well? No, I can't get well."*
>
> *"Hey, sick man by the pool, let me ask you again — do you want to get well? If you really want to get well, stop blaming other people. Stop blaming yourself. And stop worrying with that pool. Get up and walk."*

The story of the man at the pool of Bethesda illustrates, and my experience confirms, what I have come to believe: Life is Choice. This belief is almost a paradox when considered with my firmly held belief that Life is Gift. But our responsibility for the Gift of Life is something we must accept and live with. The choices I make daily shape my attitude toward circumstances beyond my control and determine what my life will be. Choices have consequences.

Wasn't it obvious that the man wanted to be healed? Why else was he there? After all, he had been paralyzed for thirty-eight long years. Probably most of his time had been spent there beside the pool waiting, longing and hoping — mostly, just waiting. Perhaps over those years something had happened to him — a lethargy he himself had failed to recognize. Life at Bethesda may have had its compensations. It may not have been altogether unpleasant to lie there in the cool porches while others his age worked in the hot, blazing sun. Some kind person must have cared for him and fed him and even clothed him.

"Do I want to be healed? What do you mean? Every time the water is stirred, someone else steps in front of me." Blame someone else. The careless driver. The doctor. The nurse. The mayor. The governor. Blame alcohol, insurance companies, inflation.

To be healthy — that is, to be whole — the man at the pool would have had to make some new choices and a radical change in the way he was living. He had grown accustomed to having poor health and complaining and just waiting.

There is, I have come to realize, a whole subculture of such waiting, illustrated by the folks who make a profession of travelling from town to town asking for handouts. I do not know what events bring them to their tragic lifestyle, but I see many of them at the church where I am pastor. These people just float around, responsible for no one — not even themselves. Churches and communities everywhere feed them, clothe them — and, when the transients' thumbs don't work — even transport them.

I've helped them, hundreds of them. They often profess to be going somewhere where they have a job, and they voluntarily promise to mail money back after they get settled, yet I've never heard from one again. It is as though they get locked into their way of life and they can't get out. Occasionally, I will ask, "Do you really want to settle down and make a home? I'll find you a job here and get you a place to stay." The response to that challenge to make a choice in favor of a life-change is often only so much foot-shuffling and squirming and hum-hawing.

In his gentle way, Jesus asked the lame man at the pool of Bethesda the same challenging question: "Do you really want to be well? Healed? Different?"

Wholeness and wellness, however, would not come to this man without a price. Nor will they come easily to us. We must desire them and seek them more than we seek anything else. We can't have everything, in spite of what we may think. Life is filled with choices and the choices come every day, sometimes in almost overwhelming numbers.

Rudyard Kipling liked to say that if we have not gotten from life what we wanted, this is proof that we did not want it, or else we tried to haggle about the price. To a limited extent, I believe that he was right. Of course, we are limited by factors in our lives which cannot be changed by any intensity of desire. There are physical limits. A blind man doesn't direct traffic. A man with no legs does not teach dancing in an Arthur Murray studio. A quadraplegic doesn't arm wrestle or run races.

What stands out as we consider the obvious need of the lame man at the pool of Bethesda and Jesus' seemingly unnecessary question is the imperative to examine what he really wanted. Did he really want to be healed or had he decided to be comfortable with his limited movement and restricted activity? How would we have answered Jesus if we had been that man?

I don't know why I should use the word *if*. That whole scene at Bethesda is an accurate symbolic representation of who we are. Certainly of who *I* am. During the month I was forced to stay in the hospital, during the three months I was under "house arrest," during eight major surgeries, and during present uncertainty, facing repeats of some of those same surgeries, I have had to ask myself, How much do I want to be healed? How willing am I to do what must be done if I am to walk again?

Pain was no doubt planned by God to alert us when all is not well, yet it is a powerful deterrent to taking steps toward healing. Current medical knowledge holds that for rehabilitation to take place, pain must be worked through.

Dependency, too, can be a dangerous deterrent to healing, especially when one has devoted and skillful caretakers. Yet the healing process requires one to become as independent as possible.

Medications, too, may deter the healing process if used unwisely.

But perhaps the most effective deterrent to healing and wholeness is the lack of will.

In one way or another, we are all little more than a bunch of cripples — lame or limping, blind or shortsighted, paralyzed or just lazy, saying we want one thing but actually wanting something else, not really interested in paying the price to change our weakened condition in life.

If we truly desire a new life with new loyalties and new priorities rather than a different sedative or better crutches, then it is possible to experience God's power and strength and a sure, confident faith like we have never experienced before! God offers a kind of wholeness that can ensure a new way of life.

Jesus said, *"Ask and it will be given you; seek*

and you will find; knock and it will be opened to you." Isaiah said, "Everyone who thirsts, come to the waters, and he who has no money, come and eat." In the letter to the Christians of Colossae the Apostle Paul wrote about being raised to life with Christ:

> Therefore, put to death those ways of thinking and acting that cause separation, sickness, loneliness . . . . Such things as self-centeredness, greed, indifference, resentment, fear — these ways of thinking and acting produce death within us and in our relationships. Bring to life those ways of thinking and acting that mean grace, healing, strength and unity in relationships. (Colossians 3:5-8)

The resources of God are placed within our reach. God doesn't offer us houses and lands; neither does he promise that if we will follow his Son, we will always enjoy good physical health and be free from the burden of suffering and live happily ever after. In spite of what some faith healers might say, Jesus didn't and doesn't heal everyone who follows Him. To be a disciple of Jesus doesn't mean we will not be sick or injured.

What *is* from God, what God *does* offer us, however, are sufficient resources for the handling of the problems of living. He offers us truth, integrity, freedom, a sense of purpose, and a sense of peace and joy that nothing can take from us. He offers to me and to you the ability to live with ourselves and our circumstances: *in whatsoever state I am therewith to be content.*

What do we really want in life? What are we after? Where are we going? In the process of careful self-examination, we will begin to discover that we are making some inner choices and once those begin to come into focus, then we can with confident faith pursue our goals with unrelenting desire.

I have served on the committee which reviews candidates for ministry in the United Methodist Church. It is a professional organization like a medical society or a bar association. In that committee we listen to the stories of candidates and probe their experiences to test their real motives for entering the ministry. Time and time again a candidate expresses this feeling: "I was not happy in my occupation. Finally I realized that I just didn't know what my goals were." Many candidates are well past thirty-five before they make decisions to change.

William Jennings Bryan said: "Destiny is not a matter of chance. It is a matter of choice."

Like the persons who frequented the pool at Bethesda, we suffer from a great number of maladies besides those that are strictly physical. Divided loyalties. Unfocused lives. Indecision. Decision is often the first step to a new life. But the choice is not always easy.

The "easy" choices are the ones to which we have to give little thought. My freedom of choice inadvertently placed me in a position where I was struck down by a car. Had I chosen to follow a different route that Saturday morning or had I chosen to leave home a bit later or a bit earlier, I would not have been at the fateful place at the fateful time. If I had chosen to stop for five seconds to tie my shoe, the car that drifted across Scenic Highway would have passed harmlessly (to me, at least) in front of me. Now, even though my choice put me at the wrong place at the wrong time, I must make another choice: the way that I respond to this circumstance. And this time I know what the ramifications are.

To complete the healing begun with excellent medical care, I must choose the way of *will*. This choice means commitment, a commitment not unlike others I have made in the past to shape my life.

When I chose the ministry as my life's work, I was buoyed by the call I experienced and by my earnest response to it. Yet achieving that goal meant hard study, times of sacrifice, and not a few frustrations. Continuing in the commitment over thirty years has meant continually centering myself on the original response. In spite of tremendous joy and huge personal gratification in the role of minister, there are daily challenges and distractions.

Susan Muto, the author of *Commitment — Key to Christian Maturity*, writes:

> *Time and again we have to choose the*

direction of our lives in the light of our divine calling. Only when we take this higher dimension into account can we commit ourselves maturely to all we are meant to be. Saying yes to what is right and having the courage to say no to what is wrong for us is a risk worth taking.

All life's commitments include risk. But so does the uncommitted life. With Susan Muto I have realized that

> *. . . if we cannot commit our lives, we may peter out. We risk living a meaningless existence, scattered and inconsistent. We may become imprisoned in the passing whims of the age. Or we find ourselves absorbed in functions that have lost the spark, the poetry of human vitality. We plod along like robots without inspiration.*

When I chose Jane as my life partner (or did *she* choose *me* first? Whatever!) neither of us knew that the choice would involve protracted re-commitment, with each of us assuming responsibility for resolving or accepting our differences. Looking back over our years together, I echo the thoughts of Buechner:

> *. . . it was within the bonds of marriage that I, for one, found a greater freedom to be and to become and to share myself than I can imagine ever having found in any other kind of relationship, and that — absurdly hopeful and poorly understood and profoundly unrealistic as the commitment was that the girl in the white dress and I made to each other in the presence, we hoped, not only of most of the people we loved best in the world, but of God as well — my life would have been incalculably diminished without it.*

Amen, I say!

If I can, with a sense of purpose and with God's help, maintain the commitments of my life choices — those made in joy and those made under duress — then, having made the choice, surely I can maintain the commitment to the fullest healing I can attain.

Some years ago we visited the Little White House in Warm Springs, Georgia. A man died there who modelled this concept: *decide what you want and then go after it.* When Franklin Delano Roosevelt was thirty-nine years old, he was crippled by polio for the rest of his life. There were many days and months of struggle and despair, and many opportunities to give up. But he didn't. Eleven years later he ran for and was elected President of the United States. One day since my accident, as I was whining a bit, Jane reminded me of President Roosevelt. She said, "Stop whining! You only have to run a church of twenty-one hundred members. President Roosevelt ran an entire nation during a World War from a wheelchair!"

I must attempt to remember every day what Susan Muto has said:

> *Gentle surrender and the inner readiness to accept as providential what God sends us strengthens us to act in accordance with the limits imposed on us by reality. We do not lay back passively and complain that "bad things always happen to good people" or that there is "nothing we can do about fate." We do not fall into the trap of believing that life is*

> *a useless passion, or that God is a kind of sadistic force raining suffering upon the innocent. Such depreciative thoughts are banished by the act of abandonment. To face courageously the shadows of pain and fear, to know that there is light at the end of even the darkest tunnel, is a mark of Christian maturity.*

I believe strongly that God has helped me during my lengthy ordeal, not the least by enabling me to make the daily — sometimes hourly — choices necessary to enhance healing. I am humbled when I read of the courageous choices of others.

Viktor Frankl, a prisoner in a Nazi concentration camp during World War II, wrote:

> *We who lived in the concentration camps remember the men who walked through the huts comforting others, giving away their last piece of bread. They may have been few in number, but they offer sufficient proof that everything can be taken from a man but one thing: the last of his freedoms — to choose*

one's   attitude   in   any   given   set   of
circumstances, to choose one's own way.

As far as I know, the unhappy woman who visited my office has not been able to change her attitude about her circumstances. My fervent hope is to be able to help her and others see the Jesus who visited Bethesda.

Do you want to be healed? Do you desire to walk again? Those were proper and insightful questions. They are questions which pierce our façades of fault-finding, of blaming others for our failing. They are questions which call upon us to examine our lives with radical honesty, which push us to focus our energies, to choose our futures.

Chapter III

Life is GRACE

After we have been given Life and when we have made choices as a part of our responding to Life, what then?

> *Listen to your life. See it for the fathomless mystery that it is. In the boredom and pain of it no less than in the excitement and gladness: touch, taste, smell your way to the holy and hidden heart of it because in the last analysis all moments are key moments, and life itself is grace.* — Frederick Buechner

The actual definition of grace has been broadened and applied to many things. In fact, the unabridged dictionary has almost a full page of definitions of "grace." But what I mean by "grace" is the meaning we can discern from the New Testament:

Grace is unmerited favor. It is the extending of favor or kindness to one who doesn't deserve it and can never earn it, favor extended simply out of the goodness of the heart of the giver.

We Americans, "self-made" individuals that we are, dislike having to accept the fact that we are saved by grace and by grace alone. We do not appreciate that God does not owe us anything or that we are left with nothing but a great humility, the thankfulness of a child who has been presented with many gifts.

By nature we are prone to want to do things for ourselves. It is not a bad trait, for this is how children become responsible and how the weak become strong. As children we say, "Mommy, let me do it myself." As grown-ups we patronize do-it-yourself hardware stores, automotive parts stores, picture-framing shops. The problem is that such a tendency toward independence can push us toward the illusion that we don't need anyone. Thank you, I can do it by myself, we naively mutter to ourselves.

For example, in pouring rain I come up to a door on crutches, having no idea how to open the door and someone asks, "Can I help?" and I say, "Oh no, I'm fine, I've got it." An illusion of self-sufficiency. The truth is we are not fine, and we don't have it. Doing it alone we don't have a clue and we don't have a chance. Our lives are more fragile than we want to admit, and in circumstances beyond our control we are dependent on the actions of others and ultimately the activity of God in our lives. We cannot cause the sun to rise in the morning. We cannot shape a baby in our hands. We cannot make someone love us. We cannot heal our bodies of disease. We cannot reverse the results of an accident.

We are much more dependent than we like to admit and life is much more precarious, uncertain, risky than we at first thought. Just when we get everything tied down and secure, it gets ripped off or ripped up in a moment.

Max Cleland was a United Methodist layman from Georgia. In 1968 an exploding grenade in Vietnam left him a triple amputee. He returned home after eighteen months of rehabilitation, entered politics, and was elected to the Georgia senate. In 1977

President Carter appointed him Director of the U.S. Veterans' Administration. Max Cleland was, according to Dr. Mark Trotter, a remarkable man, full of energy and optimism. He had a strong desire to serve. He said that his faith in God enabled him not only to survive those difficult years of hospitalization and rehabilitation but to receive a new purpose and meaning for his life. He entered the hospital in despair; he left with faith. He said that the inscription on Robert Kennedy's grave, from Aeschylus' *Agamemnon*, summarized what he learned in the hospital:

> *In our sleep, pain that cannot forget*
> *falls drop by drop*
> *Upon the heart, and in our despair*
> *against our will comes*
> *Wisdom through the awful Grace of God.*

That is a beautiful and encouraging story, told by Dr. Trotter in his book *Grace All the Way Home,* which was published in 1982. He could not have known then how the story would end. Recently Max Cleland took his own life, beat down by twenty-five years of inordinate pain and the ineffable cruelties of being a lively, intelligent person in a triple amputee's body. I cannot judge his choice to take his own life. I *can* express my own firm belief that grace was and is there for him.

Dr. Trotter, for many years a United Methodist pastor in San Diego, comments on the life experiences of many Christians: *The severity of their suffering was graced with a strange mercy.* "Strange" here indicates that the nature of such mercy is seldom recognized. Perhaps it also means that such mercy is "odd" or different from the expected — at least for most of us. Scott Peck, in *The Road Less Traveled*, wrote:

> . . . *grace [is] a common phenomenon and, to a certain extent, a predictable one. But the reality of grace will remain unexplainable within the conceptual framework of conventional science and 'natural law' as we understand it. It will remain miraculous and amazing.*

John Wesley focused on God's grace. He wrote

that God's grace works on our behalf *pre-veniently;
that is, before the event.* It works for us *in the act of
salvation,* when in conversion we become believers
and choose the Christian way. Also, it works for us *in
sanctification,* our growth in Christ-likeness.

These terms have been endlessly hashed and re-
hashed by persons looking for the deepest meanings
and the "right" way to interpret them. If we can move
past the terminology and focus on scripture, as
Wesley did, understanding brings new meaning. In
the Gospel of John we find the core of this meaning:
*For God so loved the world, that he gave his only
son, not to condemn the world, but that through him
salvation would come.*

This truth is found many times in Jesus' words:
*I have come that you might have life.
He who believes in me shall have eternal life.
When I am lifted up, I will draw all to me.*
Paul writes: *But God, who is rich in mercy, out
of the great love with which he loved us, even when
we were dead through our trespasses, made us alive
together with Christ. . . . For by grace you have*

been saved and this is not your own doing, it is the gift of God. (Ephesians 2:4-8)

The Old Testament story of the salvation of the children of Israel in the wilderness, recorded in Numbers, is a fascinating and informative one. The Hebrews had been miraculously delivered from slavery, the waters of the Red Sea parting for them to escape the charging Egyptian soldiers, and Moses had received the Commandments instructing the Hebrews how to live for generations yet to come. And then, the Bible says, before they entered the Promised Land to receive their inheritance, God reminded them that their lives were and always would be dependent upon him.

He taught them this truth in a very dramatic way. As they traveled, many of them began to complain about their condition — too hot in the sun and too cold at night, too windy, too little food and hardly any water. "Why are we here?" some asked. The writer of Numbers says, *He sent snakes among them*.

HE SENT SNAKES. Slippery, slimy, big poisonous snakes. Had I been Moses I would have pleaded with God, "Not snakes — please, not snakes. Anything — gnats, gators, rats, even inflation or higher taxes, but not snakes!"

The snakes in the wilderness struck down many of the Hebrews, and God told Moses how they could be cured: make a bronze serpent and place it high on a pole; then let the people look up to it when they are bitten.

We don't understand the magical mystery of these healings, but we can now look back and realize that when the Hebrews looked up at the bronze snake, they were reminded once again that their freedom and their future, their health and healing, came from God — he who has created us, has instructed us, has delivered us and is redeeming us.

Later after Jesus died, generation after generation would learn to look up to him to find their salvation, their health, their true happiness. Jesus died a death as total and completely hopeless as any man or woman has ever died or will ever die. He died to show us that, in the end, no aspect of the life experience is empty of God's grace. We are reminded by both the lifted-up, bronze serpent and the bloody cross that our lives hang by the slender thread of divine grace.

When trouble comes, when the snakes strike, we must look up, for it is God who can and will do for us what we cannot do for ourselves. "My grace is sufficient for you." He has given us the word. Sufficient. Sufficient means an adequate amount, enough, as much as is needed.

When one of the oil-rich Arab kings decided to replace all of his fleet of automobiles with new Rolls-Royces purchased from England, one of the underlings wrote to the Rolls-Royce Corporation asking for specifics of the model. When the reply came back, it was noticed that the company didn't specify the amount of horsepower, so a second inquiry was made. In typical British understatement came the reply: "In regards to your inquiry concerning the horsepower of the Rolls-Royce automobile, let us say do not worry. It is adequate."

Christian people have experienced the truth of this assuring promise for over two thousand years. In this most unusual year of my life journey I have found it to be true in my own experience. God's grace is sufficient, is enough, is adequate for facing the trials and tribulations of every day. Even when persons do not acknowledge their creator, our God of love is working on their behalf.

So in facing the difficulties of this and every day, regardless of the immensity of the problems which we may face, remember the reply of the Rolls-Royce Company. "Do not worry; God's grace is adequate!"

Jesus relied on this truth when at the beginning of his ministry he was tempted to misuse his power. He could have turned stones into bread in the wilderness. He could have jumped safely from the pinnacle of the temple. He could have assumed ownership of all he surveyed from the high mountain. It must have been very tempting, as he began to realize the abilities and power which were at his disposal, to use such power to accomplish his earthly purpose. His task was clear, to communicate the nature of God to a world at odds with God's nature. If he had taken the position that the end justified the means, he could have used the miraculous power at his fingertips to force the love of God into a hateful people. Yet with his understanding of who he was and with God's grace he was able to resist the temptation.

The passage describing Jesus' lonely struggle is an apocryphal narrative, illustrating the classic conflict between humankind and evil. The Apostle Paul knew that the people of his day experienced the need for being "saved from" the conflicts that evil brings to life. He offered the people of Ephesus something to be "saved to":

> . . . by Grace you have been saved and given abundant life and the sure promise of Eternal life, and this is not your own doing, it is the gift of God. In Christ today you can start all over again. Behold the old has passed and the new has come. (Ephesians 2:8,9)

If Jesus and the Apostles needed God's grace, so also do we who live in a much different world. I don't believe the people of biblical times could have imagined the power of current technologies, political systems, and the wealth distribution of the twentieth century. People of every generation are tempted to misuse power, authority, or materialism — and so are we. I've seen power and wealth destroy more people than I have seen it make strong the character of people. Jesus' temptation is everyman's story, even in our time. There is nothing new.

The Gospel writers end the narrative with a tantalizing comment: "And the angels came and ministered unto him." What a comforting message! After our struggles, God in his grace provides peace.

Jesus chose to reject the tempter's alluring offer and to take the way of the trusting servant. His choice led ultimately to his resurrection. Well, it may be said, it led first to his crucifixion. Oh, no! The crucifixion — pain and suffering — occurs to us all in varying degrees. Some handle it and others don't. But those who move through crucifying experiences to the resurrection live lives of trusting faith in the sufficiency of God's grace.

For many of us there is a hesitancy to accept that gift of grace. This reluctance is illustrated by an experience described by Kim Wilson in a recent issue of *The Lutheran.* Anyone who has travelled in the Middle East, she writes, is familiar with the persistence of people selling everything from postcards to relics. One day in an Arab country a woman in a tattered, flowing robe followed her down the street, speaking softly but urgently. Employing all the tricks a seasoned traveler learns, Kim avoided eye contact and shook her head repeatedly as the woman spoke first in Arabic, then other languages, seeking a means of communication. Blocking the path, she pulled a rock from a weathered pouch. The rock's rose luster caught the sun, brightly shimmering in her brown palm. Leery of a street deal, Kim felt increasingly exasperated, but the Arab woman's determination never wavered.

At last the woman tried German, urgently insisting, "*Geschenk! Geschenk!* " And finally Kim understood. *Geschenk* . . . gift.

Her fear of being cheated had prevented Kim from seeing the Arab woman as a gift-giver. Her preconceived notions, her lack of understanding, had left no room for such a possibility.

In the same way, our fears and pre-conceived notions can prevent us from recognizing and accepting God's gracious gift to us. Only when we change our expectations, only when we begin to listen for the Word he has provided, can we understand.

Gift.

The gift is life.

Life is gift.

Epilogue

So once it would have been—'tis so no more;
I have submitted to a new control:
A Power is gone, which nothing can restore;
A deep distress hath humanized my Soul.

Not for a moment could I now behold
A smiling sea, and be what I have been:
The feeling of my loss will ne'er be old;
This, which I know, I speak with mind serene.

— William Wordsworth

Since that painful morning in September I find, myself, that the experience of deep distress has indeed "humanized" my soul. The result is that I experience a new awareness of the pain of individuals who suffer, so acute that I have to turn away from magazine photographs that depict people who are hurting, and glance away when television news and dramatic programs show people hurt or beaten or murdered. When I am aware that someone is going into surgery or having a long hospital stay, whereas once I might have casually accepted it as the way things are, I do so no longer.

I have been intrigued for some time with the way Mother Teresa and her followers, who minister to the poor and needy, identify with them and experience the presence of Christ. With my new sense of identification with those who suffer, I have been placed in touch with a dimension of the love of God that I had never personally experienced before.

The day I last ran along Escambia Bay, enjoying Wordsworth's "smiling sea," my body received a severe blow, and my soul began that humanizing experience.

I intend to run again, but the "feeling of my loss will ne'er grow old." If, now, I speak from a "mind serene," it is because I know three things:

✤

Life is gift. And I embrace it, even with infirmities — perhaps because of them.

Life is choice. And I choose it — along with the responsibilities and commitments which choice entails.

Life is grace. And I accept it — with humility and gratitude.

✤✤✤✤

NOTES

11,12 Franz Lidz, *Sports Illustrated*, May 16, 1994.

12,13,42,47   Frederick Buechner, *Listening To Your Life* (New York, HarperCollins Publishers).

19,20 Andrew Young, *A Way Out Of No Way* (Nashville, Thomas Nelson Publishers).

20, 21 M. Scott Peck, *Further Along The Road Less Traveled* (New York, Simon & Schuster).

24,25 Terry Waite, *Taken On Trust* (New York, Harcourt Brace & Company).

30,31 Joe Elmore, *This Fleeting Instant* (Pensacola, Ardara House, Publishers).

40,41,43,44 Susan Muto, *Commitment — Key to Christian Maturity* (New York, Paulist Press).

44,45   Viktor Frankl, *Man's Search for Meaning* (New York, Washington Square Press).

50,51 Mark Trotter, *Grace All the Way Home* (Nashville, The Upper Room).

51 M. Scott Peck, *The Road Less Traveled* (New York, Simon & Schuster).

59 Kim Wilson, "What Do You Have For Me Today?", *The Lutheran*, July, 1994.

61 William Wordsworth, *Elegiac Stanzas, Suggested by a picture of Peele Castle, In A Storm, Painted by Sir George Beaumont.*